Praise for *Life on a 3x5*

"*Life on a 3x5: A Framework for Daily Success* is an excellent tool and is easy to use. A few minutes a day and I'm on my way."

**David Tillman,
IBM Consultant**

"I purchased the *Life on a 3x5: A Framework for Daily Success* book with the hope that *something* would help me organize my thoughts. What a wonderfully simple plan, I can't wait to get started! Thanks, Scotty, for sharing this with all of us."

Chariti Kupiec

"I've had the *Life on a 3x5* book (it was originally an e-book only) for seven years now. I can honestly say that applying these simple practices has allowed me to get more done in less time and focus on what matters most."

Ashton McIntyre

"*Life on a 3x5: A Framework for Daily Success* has been transformational for me. It helped me define and clarify my life's purpose, pursue and accomplish goals, develop disciplines, and set priorities. I believe this book will have a lasting impact on your life."

Colonel Tim Cole, USMC (Ret.)

"I never imagined that a simple system would have such a profound impact on my creativity and productivity. I encourage you to implement *Life on a 3x5* as you begin your day."

**Kyle Cunningham,
Nonprofit Executive**

LIFE on a 3x5

A Framework for Daily Success by
Scotty Sanders

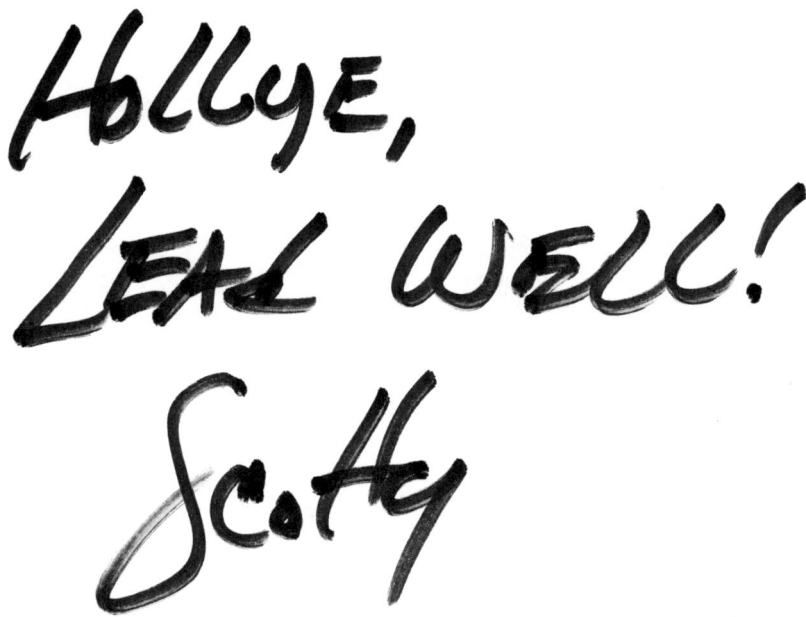

Life on a 3x5: A Framework for Daily Success

Copyright ©2020 Scotty Sanders

Copyright covers all content in this publication. All rights reserved.

No part of this publication may be reproduced, stored, or transmitted in any form by any means, whether graphic, electronic, photocopying, mechanical, recording, or otherwise. Expressly for personal use only, not for financial gain.

Visual design and publishing support by Kevin Lynam
www.TheImageDoctor.net

ISBN: 978-1-645-50883-0

Dedication

This book is dedicated to my dad, Louis Sanders.

He is my greatest hero.

Acknowledgments

To my wife, Cindy, thank you for always being by my side on any project. We work as a team. Your contributions to the book are important, but most of all, I am thankful for your belief in me.

My creative director, Kevin Lynam makes everything I do sound and look better. I am grateful for your friendship!

Contents

Foreword by Col. Tim Cole, USMC (Ret.) xi
Introduction 1
    1—Who Needs a Framework of Success? 3
    2—The Story Behind This Book 5
    3—Stop Being Robbed! 7
    4—Details of the Plan 13
    5—Write It Down 17
Creating Your Own 3x5 21
    6—Step One: Purpose 23
    7—Step Two: Passion 31
    8—Step Three: Goals 37
    9—Step Four: Daily Disciplines 47
    10—Step Five: Priorities 53
    11—Step Six: Gratitude 59
    12—3x5 in Review 65

—FOREWORD—
Colonel Tim Cole, USMC (Ret.)

"Our modern-day, information-driven world of 24-hour news cycles, social media distractions, shortened attention spans, and personal yearnings for a more balanced life of personal relationships and vocation success can quickly consume our waking hours. There is hope! Author Scotty Sanders' *Life on a 3x5: A Framework for Daily Success* provides a proven, simple 6-step process to help us clarify, focus, and begin living our best lives now—deliberately.

I met Scotty Sanders several years ago during a time of significant life change. Following my post 9-11 years of military duty assignments and overseas deployments away from my family, my wife and I returned home to our five adult children, their spouses, and our grandchildren. Joyful in reuniting with family, I was challenged in my transition from a highly successful Marine Corps career into an unfamiliar world of entrepreneurship and personal business ownership. I found in Scotty Sanders an experienced and highly successful business owner; a valued, respected leader in both for-profit and nonprofit sectors; a prolific, best-selling author; an eager and constant lifelong learner; an engaging and encouraging friend; and a cherished mentor. Scotty shared with me this same six step process early in our friendship, and I've utilized its elements effectively to my great benefit. Now, this simple, easily implementable process is available to you as well as your family, friends, and business colleagues via Scotty Sanders' newest book release *Life on a 3x5: A Framework for Daily Success*.

The 3x5 methodology has been transformational for me, defining and clarifying my life's purpose, living my purpose with passion, pursuing and accomplishing goals via developed disciplines and priority setting. In the new decade ahead, I will continue with renewed zeal in this process! I've also shared my experience and personal benefit of this methodology among other business associates, and they were always eager to implement it themselves and share it with their team.

Today, I have genuine gratitude for my friend and mentor Scotty Sanders and his lasting impact in my life. I believe this book and its effective process will become beneficial in your life. Learn, live, love, and serve!"

—**Colonel Tim Cole,
USMC Retired**

31-year "Mustang" Marine Corps Colonel Tim Cole served during the terms of five US presidents and deployed around the world in both war and peace, earning numerous military decorations. Today, Colonel Cole honors our military Veterans—expertly guiding family and friends through research, historical context, understanding, and recognition—honoring a beloved Veteran's military service and bringing healing along with honor.

Introduction

My passion is to empower the next generation. Because of that passion, I wrote *Quest of the Keys*, a book that teaches character development.

One of my favorite characters in the book is the elder of Leonesse. As the elder was meeting with his students one day, he shared a story about Mr. Eckhardt, the wealthiest man to ever live in Leonesse.

Mr. Eckhardt had a beautiful daughter who became engaged to a young man who built houses. Mr. Eckhardt wanted to know his future son-in-law better, so he made a request. "I want you to build the finest house in all of Leonesse. Spare no expense. Make sure you use nothing but the very best, the best workers and the best materials."

The young man could not believe his good fortune. He was marrying a beautiful girl and now was going to build the signature home in Leonesse. Periodically, Mr. Eckhardt would meet with the young man and ask him the same questions: "Are you using the best workers? Are you using the best materials?" The young man answered, "Yes, sir, nothing but the best."

Although the young man told Mr. Eckhardt he would do his best, soon, he began to cut corners in his work, knowing no one would ever find out. He thought he could save time and make an even more substantial profit.

The big day arrived, and the house was complete. As the young man handed the key to Mr. Eckhardt, his future father-in-law asked the young man once again, "Did you use nothing but the best?"

He answered, "Yes, sir, nothing but the very best." Next, Mr. Eckhardt did something quite surprising. He handed the key back to the young man and said, "I want you and my daughter to live in the finest house in all of Leonesse."

The lesson in this story is that each of us is building our own house. When you do less than your best or take advantage of others, you may think you are getting ahead, but in truth, you are hurting yourself. The reality is you are building your own house.

I share this story because as you begin learning the steps for daily success, it is up to you.

When you own your story, you get to write the ending.

What kind of ending do you want?

What kind of house do you want to build?

— 1 —

Who Needs a Framework of Success?

Do you wonder about your purpose in life? What about goals and priorities? Do you look for ways to direct and affect your present and your future?

This book can help!

Benefits of a Daily Plan

Keeping a log of your daily thoughts and plans has been proven to:

- Manage anxiety
- Reduce stress
- Cope with depression

—2—
The Story Behind This Book

I have trained and advised thousands of people on how to embrace and develop a plan for personal growth. Some listened, tried it for a while, and then gave up. Others have taken my advice and had great success, but my best guess is less than 10% have genuinely followed through.

Deep down, I believe we all have good intentions to grow on many levels. Unfortunately, life happens to us so quickly; most people never devote the time and discipline necessary to work on improving themselves.

What about YOU...will you stick with it?

Your continued personal growth and development is a fundamental process that continually prepares you to meet the upcoming challenges of life and achieve your full potential every day. But a process is nothing without a plan—and this book gives you a terrific starting point for lifelong success.

Have you ever written in a diary or journal? This plan is similar, but with a clear and simple format. I prefer using a pen and a 3x5 index card to plan my work and work my plan, but a smartphone, tablet, or computer works as well.

Ready to roll? Let's go!

—3—
Stop Being Robbed!

Distractions are robbing you of valuable time and productivity. Focus has never been more important yet harder to attain. Consider all the ways distractions are attacking you at home, school, or work. Recognize these dangers, and learn to control your attention.

Does this scenario describe your life? Upon waking in the morning, you turn on your phone to check emails, and ten minutes pass. You decide to check Facebook and Twitter, and thirty minutes are gone. Not to mention the funny YouTube video and others that pop up on the side. Before you know it, your morning is gone, and you have accomplished nothing; you have been robbed!

Life on a 3x5

> **The #1 skill to stop distractions in life is learning to control your attention!**

Your attention is an asset, and what captures your attention controls your life. Many leaders are busy being busy. In reality, they are underachieving. Each one of you has so much potential! The sad truth is most people do not realize their potential because of distraction.

How do you begin making a change? Start by conducting an audit of how you currently spend your time. Identify distractions and gaps in time where you are unproductive.

- Do you stay on your phone constantly? Did you know the average adult sends over 100 text messages each day?

- Do you check social media sites throughout the day? The average person spends up to two hours a day on social media sites.

- Do you sit on the couch and watch TV every evening? The average American watches up to five hours of TV every day.

How Can You Stop Being Robbed by Distraction?

Organize Your Day
Begin your day with 14 minutes (approximately 1% of your day) devoted to gathering your thoughts and prioritizing what you need to get done. Define your Top 3 Goals/Top 3 Priorities of the day.

Check Email
Do not check your email all throughout the day. Add email items to your task list or set specific times to check your email and respond accordingly (example: first thing in the morning, after lunch, and before you leave work for the day).

Get Lost
Do you have that coworker who stops by your office to chat, and thirty minutes pass? Does your phone demand your attention with constant messages, texts, notifications, etc.? Shut your door, silence your phone, and turn off notifications. Stop making yourself available to distractions.

Try the Two-Minute Rule
Entrepreneur Steve Olenski says to implement the "two-minute rule" by completing any task that comes up if it can be done in two minutes or less. Immediately knocking off these tasks can take less time than making a note to come back to them later in the day.

Declutter
Prepare a clean, uncluttered space to accomplish a task. An organized, neat workspace can improve productivity.

Focus
Stick to a task until it is complete. Multitasking has been proven to make you lose time and productivity. According to a Harvard Study, our minds wander nearly 50% of the time. Practice the 360 Laser: 3 times a day, block 60 minutes of uninterrupted, super-focused time.

Goals
Identify your goals, and make them your priority throughout the day. Push distracting thoughts out of your head by reminding yourself what you are supposed to be doing.

Take Breaks
Take a short break for a few minutes if you are having difficulty focusing. Work hard for 50 minutes and take a ten-minute break to refocus. It is also a good idea to eat lunch away from your desk. Even if you don't leave work, eat lunch at another spot in your office. You will return from your break and be ready to work.

You control your calendar. You control your schedule. You make a choice to *stop being robbed*!

A SIMPLE PLAN:

Take 1% of your day (14 minutes) to plan the other 99% of your day, and the other 99% will go better!

Benefits of Planning:

- Greatly reduces stress

- Gives you peace of mind by formulating steps of action to accomplish your goals

- Helps you prepare for obstacles and gain a sense of control over your life

- Helps you resolve problems, fears, and concerns

- Provides an opportunity for self-talk and identification of negative behaviors/thoughts

- Gains control of your emotions and mental health

—4—

Details of the Plan

I knew the criteria for *Life on a 3x5* had to be simple. Also, I wanted to capture this plan concisely to share with others.

Criteria

Simple: Anything too difficult will not last.

Concise: Other plans are too wordy or vague.

Effective: This method has worked for me and many others. Also, research shows the concepts are *very* effective.

Doable: Anyone can do it.

Repeatable: It can be used year after year.

Bonuses

Clarity: Begin each day being clear on what is important.

Focus: This plan will help you focus like a laser.

Good Results: If you follow the plan, I am confident you will have improved results.

Research

The Power of Three

A phrase I have heard through leadership circles for the last several years is the "Power of Three." Research proves that our mind can handle three thoughts very well, but when adding a fourth, it causes confusion, and procrastination occurs.

Research also shows how significant it is to write plans/goals down on paper. If you have doubts, look at the Harvard study taken several years ago. Here is the short version:

The Harvard MBA graduates who had goals/plans but did not write them down had an income of twice as much as the MBAs that did not have any goals. The MBA graduates who had goals/plans that **were written down** had an income of 10 times greater than those of the classmates that did not have goals/plans.

Details of the Plan

Only 3% of the Harvard MBA students had goals and wrote them down, and their income was ten times higher than the others.

—5—
Write It Down

Over the years, I have used smartphones, tablets, and laptops to take notes and keep up with my personal growth plan. However, I have found that none of these tools is more effective than the physical act of writing on paper. I did some more homework to verify this wasn't merely a type of "Scotty weird thing."

New research is showing the importance of writing things down. Brain imaging studies show that writing causes higher brain activity called the RAS or "Reticular Activating System."

Writing triggers the RAS and then sends a signal to the cerebral cortex to focus on what a person deems as most important at that moment.

Writing Things Down

- Improves memory

- Makes a permanent record

- Shows you are serious

- Makes you more accountable

- Helps you work through thoughts better

*If you're constantly on your phone or tablets, you may prefer to use the "notes" app to record your plans. Just remember to use a new note every day, and make yourself do the action of typing each item each day!

Helpful Hints

Must-have tools for *Life on a 3x5*:

- Pen

- 3x5 index cards or notebook

- Smartphone, tablet, or computer

Many concepts from *Life on a 3x5* are covered in greater detail in *Quest of the Keys,* a fantasy fiction self-help narrative, also by Scotty Sanders.

Visit www.QuestOfTheKeys.com for ordering information.

3x5 Example Front:

1/22/20

PURPOSE: To encourage and empower others to live, lead, and finish well.

PASSIONS: 1) Learning, 2) Developing Leaders, 3) The Next Generation

YEARLY GOALS: 1) 20 Speaking Engagements, 2) Fundraising $250K, 3) 2,500 One Focus

3x5 Example Back:

DAILY DISCIPLINES:
1) Study, 2) Plan, 3) Write

PRIORITIES:
1) One-on-Ones, 2) Proof book, 3) Vet Auditor

GRATITUDE:
1) My 21,915th day and counting, 2) Board members, 3) Mastermind Group

Creating Your Own 3x5

We have all heard of the KISS principle:

- Keep
- It
- Super
- Simple

(KEEP IT SUPER SIMPLE), a practice implemented by the U.S. Navy. The KISS principle states that most systems work best if they are kept simple rather than made complex. *Life on a 3x5* is designed for ultimate simplicity and maximum success.

Just follow the simple instructions, and see results!

—6—

Step One: Purpose

> "Efforts and courage
> are not enough without
> purpose and direction."
>
> **John F. Kennedy**

I was cut from the basketball team in my last year of middle school. Don't feel sorry for me yet, because this was a life-changing experience and led me to find my purpose in life!

Life on a 3x5

I grew up in a family of four boys. Since we were young, playing sports was our top priority. I was known as an athlete and was embarrassed and hurt when I didn't make the team. I wasn't the only one surprised; word spread quickly.

Two weeks later, the coach called me into his office. He said, "Scotty, I'm sorry I had to cut you from the team. The truth is you are not very good. You can't dribble, you are not very tall, and you can't really shoot the basketball." Side note: Are you wondering if I am feeling better yet?

Then the coach said something I will never forget. "The last two weeks of practice, the team has no hustle, their play is sloppy, and they are lacking execution. I talked to a couple of players to find out what was wrong, and they said, 'We need Scotty back on the team.'" Then the coach admitted he said to them, "Scotty is not a very good basketball player." The boys said, "Coach, we don't need him on the team because he is a good basketball player, we need him because he is a good leader. He challenges us and makes us a better team."

That day, the coach asked me a question. "Scotty, would you be willing to come back on the team, knowing you will probably never play? Also, I want you to promise to work harder and give your all to the team." Now, this would make a much better story if I told you I joined the team and had an incredible season. Here is the reality.

I sat on the bench until the last game of the season, and the only reason I played was that many of my teammates were sick. They needed a fifth player. Had I thought I was on the team to be the star player, I would have been disappointed. However, I knew my purpose was to make everyone else on the team better. That experience gave me insight into my purpose in life.

By the way: I have something in common with Michael Jordan—he got cut from his basketball team. He became the greatest player of all time. Michael's purpose was to become a sports icon that transformed basketball. For me, it was to help others achieve success in life.

Another side note: I wonder how many of my junior high school basketball players have been invited by the Dallas Mavericks organization to speak to a group of leaders before their basketball game?

My purpose statement is to encourage and empower others to live, lead, and finish well. I fulfill my purpose in professional speaking, international leadership training, or when I am writing a book such as *Life on a 3x5*.

Answer these questions to give insight into your life purpose:

1. What can you do to change the world?

_____

_____

_____

_____

_____

_____

2. At the end of your life, what do you want to be remembered for?

_____

_____

_____

_____

_____

_____

_____

3. What are your strengths and abilities?

_____

_____

_____

_____

_____

_____

_____

_____

4. What are your deepest values?

5. Write out on paper what you believe to be your purpose. Until you know your purpose, you will always lack the clarity you need to live life to its fullest.

6. Write your purpose statement. Try to keep it simple—within one sentence. Write your purpose statement on your 3x5 card each day.

For more information on how to write your purpose statement, read *Quest of the Keys* pp. 32–35.

> "It is much easier to
> write your life purpose.
>
> The greater challenge
> is to live it each day."
>
> **Quest of the Keys**

Benefits of Purpose

Purpose requires both a personal desire to accomplish something meaningful to ourselves and commitment to take the actions needed to do so. Research shows that teens and young adults who seek purpose report higher life satisfaction and levels of happiness. New research even suggests that a feeling of purpose in young people is associated with better physical health.

> "True happiness...is not attained
> through self-gratification
> but through fidelity to a
> worthy purpose."
>
> **Helen Keller**

—7—

Step Two: Passion

"Nothing is as important as passion.
No matter what you want to do in
your life, be passionate."

Jon Bon Jovi

My dad lives a life of passion. As of this writing, he is 85 years old and still works full-time selling insurance. Over the past ten years, he has finished either first, second, or third in top sales of a company with thousands of salespeople. Why? Because he is passionate about what he does. Passion is like a superpower. When you find out what you were made to do, you feel like you can change the world!

I was speaking to a group of high school seniors a few years ago. Afterward, I talked to many of the young men and women as they asked me to sign their *Quest of the Keys* book. I asked one young man what his plans were after high school. He said, "I want to be a fireman." I told him it was a very noble profession and a great way to serve his community. Then I asked, "What led you to this decision?" His answer caught me by surprise. The young man said, "My best friend's dad is a fireman, and I found out they get great insurance and can retire before they are fifty-five years old."

Now, let me ask you; do you want your goal in life to retire before you are fifty-five years old? The other choice is to be like my dad and live life to the fullest, being productive, helping people, and doing something you love for as long as you can? It's called *passion*!

Passion

All of us have unique gifts to offer the world. How do you find your passion? One way is to follow your excitement and take action to the best of your ability. Finding your passion takes work—you cannot just sit and think about what makes you feel excited!

1. Passion is the first step to significance.

2. A passion to help others will change you.

3. Living with passion will make you a more productive and dedicated person.

4. All things are possible with passion.

5. Passion will take up the slack in other areas of your life.

Answering these questions will give insight into your passion:

1. What excites you about the world?

_____
_____
_____
_____
_____
_____
_____
_____
_____
_____
_____
_____
_____
_____

2. If you had to teach something, what would you teach?

_____

_____

_____

_____

_____

_____

_____

3. What makes you cry?

_____

_____

_____

_____

_____

_____

_____

_____

Step Two: Passion

4. What makes you angry?

5. What activities make you lose track of time?

Life on a 3x5

6. Write three things you are passionate about. These should connect back to your purpose. Write these on your 3x5 card each day.

_____

_____

_____

_____

_____

For more information about passion, read *Quest of the Keys* pp. 37–51.

"Passion is something that will consume your thoughts and time."

Quest of the Keys

—8—

Step Three: Goals

"By recording your dreams and goals on paper, you set in motion the process of becoming the person you most want to be. Put your future in good hands—your own."

Mark Victor Hansen

If you remember from an earlier story, I grew up in a family of four boys. My brother Casey was the youngest of the four. While my other two brothers and I matured faster, Casey was small for his age. No one wanted him on their team when we played sports with the neighbors. Of course, we picked on him because he was not a fast runner or strong enough to wrestle any of us.

Casey got tired of being the smallest and weakest of the neighborhood. He started running, doing push-ups and sit-ups. Growing older, he began lifting weights, increasing the pounds and repetitions. He set goals for weight training. Casey transformed into a bigger, stronger kid. He practiced something I call "Big is little and little is big."

Most people think it is one big thing we do to achieve success, but it is the little things we do consistently over time. Little becomes big with discipline.

Several years went by, and Casey continued to work out with amazing results. He had goals, wrote them down, and measured his progress. At 19 years old, he was recognized as the strongest teenager in the world as an All-American Powerlifter.

After college, Casey became a strength-and-conditioning coach for a local high school and won several state championships in football and one national championship. Casey was also recognized as the top high school strength coach in the U.S. by the National Football League.

Casey passed down his goal-setting to his family. He and his wife Sharon have four boys: one is an orthopedic surgeon, another played for LSU winning a national championship (he now works for a pharmaceutical company). Their next son is an emergency room doctor and the youngest is in dental school.

> **Your potential is one thing;
> what you do with it is quite another!**

Let's Talk About Goals

In my digital training course, *Life on a 3x5: A Framework for Daily Success*, there is an entire section on goals. My goals are a part of my daily plan. Each day, I write down my Top 3 Goals on a 3x5 index card, imprinting their importance on my brain.

Studies have shown less than 5% of people have goals. Less than 3% write them down each day, and less than 1% of those goals pass the S.M.A.R.T. test.

For simplification, I will refer to my goal-setting framework as the "1 Percenters" because less than 1% will set goals this way.

My 4 Essentials for the "1 Percenters"

1. Have three goals that flow from your purpose statement.

2. Pass the S.M.A.R.T. test:

    » **S** – Specific

    » **M** – Measurable

    » **A** – Attainable (Use my Goal Stretcher Formula™ — reaching goals with a stretch) For example:
    - Goal 1 has approximately 25% attainability
    - Goal 2 has approximately 50% attainability
    - Goal 3 has approximately 75% attainability

    » **R** – Relevant (ties back to your purpose)

    » **T** – Time-Sensitive (annual)

3. Write your three goals on a 3x5 card daily.

4. Use lag measures and lead measures. Your goals are lag measures, meaning certain activities must happen to attain your goals. Those activities are lead measures.

Example: In 2019, my Goal Number 1 was to raise $250k for my nonprofit *Quest of the Keys*. As my number-one-goal, there was only a 25% probability I would reach it; in other words, it was going to be a stretch.

Goal-setting, when done right, is a powerful tool. Specific, measurable goals give much-needed focus to your energy and passion.

In addition to having S.M.A.R.T. goals, your goals need to have "lead measures." For example, if one of your goals is to lose weight, is that a goal? No! It is not S.M.A.R.T. Here is how you make losing weight a S.M.A.R.T. goal:

My goal is to lose 30 pounds in the next year.

- ☐ Is it specific? Yes
- ☐ Measurable? Yes
- ☐ Attainable? Yes
- ☐ Relevant? Yes
- ☐ Time-sensitive? Yes

Using the above goal of losing 30 pounds, here are the "lead measures."

Goal: Lose 30 pounds.

Here are some examples of lead measures:

- Exercise 45 minutes a day, three days a week.

- Limit desserts to once a week.

- Drink 64 oz. of water a day.

- Eat according to my preset plan and have fried food no more than twice a month.

Review your lead measures daily/weekly. If you are not moving toward your goal, adjust the lead measures. Remember, goals cause us to stretch. They should be challenging us to do more than usual.

It has been said the only bad goal is one set too low for a challenge.

Some Examples of Goals:

- Increase sales by 20%

- Reduce customer complaints by 50%

- Have a date night with your spouse weekly

- Read 10 books

- Lose 30 pounds

- Launch two new products

Step Three: Goals

Goals are critical steps we take on the path to our dreams.

Goals

Goals are tools that require daily discipline. The power of goals lies in the direction, focus, and accountability they provide.

1. They can move us from mediocre maintenance to a worthy destination.

2. They present a challenge that will help us stretch beyond the ordinary.

3. They present a clear picture of where we want to go and how we plan to get there.

4. They provide a focus, which is especially important in today's world.

5. When we reach goals, we are encouraged to set new goals for the future.

Write your Top 3 Goals for the next twelve months. They should be S.M.A.R.T. (Specific, Measurable, Attainable, Relevant and Time-sensitive), and you should review them regularly.

Step Three: Goals

These ideas will help you get started with goal-setting:

1. List three books you will read in the next ninety days.

_____

_____

_____

_____

_____

_____

2. List two ways you will make a healthy change in your eating habits in the next ninety days.

_____

_____

_____

_____

_____

_____

3. List three changes you will make in your regular routine that include getting more exercise (example: parking your car farther from your destination).

_____

_____

_____

_____

_____

_____

Write three daily goals on your 3 x 5 card each day. It is okay to have more than three goals, and I generally do, but for *Life on a 3 x 5*, three is all you need!

For more information about goals, read *Quest of the Keys* pp. 96–97.

— 9 —

Step Four: Daily Disciplines

"Success is nothing more than a few simple disciplines practiced every day."

Jim Rohn

To the Himalayas and Back: Discipline

Several years ago, a good friend of mine named Ed approached me about going on an Extreme Mission Trip to the Himalayan Mountains. I had gone with Ed on mission trips to Honduras in the past, and they had been physically challenging. This trip was much more rigorous, requiring eight months of training. I asked myself this question, "What is my level of discipline?"

The definition of discipline is control gained by obedience. As a consultant and speaker, I often discuss the subject of taking control of our lives. The question is can you take control of your life without discipline? I don't believe that is possible.

The first goal I had was to train for hiking four to five hours at a time with fifty pounds on my back. After buying my gear, I worked my way up from walking with an empty backpack to filling it with a large landscape rock from our flower bed. I carried the rock in my backpack while I walked and, eventually, did the stair climber at my gym. After only a few minutes on the stair climber, I was very fatigued. A good friend and manager of the club asked a question I will never forget: "So, how much weight do you have in your backpack?"

I answered, "I'm not sure, but it has to be close to fifty pounds." He suggested I weigh it on the scales and I agreed, wanting to show off my prowess. To my dismay, the scales said that rock weighed thirteen pounds. Could this be some joke? Could the scales be broken? Thirty-seven pounds to go? I thought, *This is impossible.*

I had set a goal and thought I was disciplined, but I was missing the mark. I had to ask myself another question: is this my true level of discipline? A follow-up question would be "Can this be done better?"

Step Four: Daily Disciplines

You may be wondering if I made it to the Himalayas and back. I did. I experienced challenges I could not have borne had I not been physically and mentally prepared for the trip. I have heard it said that success in any undertaking requires constant improvement! The same applies to your level of discipline.

Discipline

A disciplined person

- clearly defines their goals
- eliminates excuses
- takes responsibility
- is true to their word
- takes care of themselves
- sets boundaries
- revels in routine
- leads with their mind over mood
- works at developing habits

Scotty's Three Daily Disciplines:

Study

Plan

Write

Answering these questions will help you with your daily disciplines:

1. What are some daily disciplines you have in your life that lead back to your purpose? List as many as possible.

Step Four: Daily Disciplines

2. Write down three "big-picture disciplines" that you will do each day. (These are different than daily tasks. Your daily disciplines are "bigger-picture" actions. For example, one of my three daily disciplines is to study. Each day, I study 30 minutes to 5 hours. These three disciplines will not change each day). After you have identified your Three Daily Disciplines, write these each day on your 3 x 5 card.

_____

_____

_____

_____

_____

_____

_____

_____

_____

(I suggest you create a weekly "to-do list" on a separate document. This is where you list the various tasks you will accomplish throughout the week. A typical week for me is 20–25 tasks. Ideally, each task is benefit oriented, not merely busywork to fill up space on a page. That may not always be possible, and there's always room for fun things on your list of tasks. Just try to think in bigger pictures.)

—10—
Step Five: Priorities

> "The key is not to prioritize what's on your schedule, but to schedule your priorities."
>
> **Stephen Covey**

The opportunity cost of spending one dollar today is ten dollars you could have had in retirement. In fact, this single concept is the cornerstone of billionaire Warren Buffett's vast fortune. He recognized the idea when he was ten years old, and it has guided his decisions ever since.

Opportunity costs can also relate to priorities. Decisions typically involve constraints such as time, resources, rules, etc. Doing one thing often means you cannot do something else (priorities).

Example:

An IT worker is offered a new job with a higher salary in a city with a lower quality of life. The opportunity cost of the higher salary is a higher quality of life. A decision must be made, therefore prioritizing the situation.

How to Prioritize
Life's most important question: WIN?

What's

Important

Now?

This question can serve as a guide to help you prioritize the choices and decisions you are faced with every day. You have an opportunity to waste your life, spend your life, or invest your life!

We all have things in life we say are important to us, but our actions show something different. This advice is going to sound simple, but it can be life changing.

Learn to schedule your priorities!

Each day, I write down my three top priorities on a 3x5 index card. By focusing on the three most important items and completing them, I can ensure my day was a success.

There will always be distractions during the day, but by putting these priorities on paper and scheduling time to complete them, you are set up for great success.

Often, we must do things we may not want to do, but they are part of our job. As you consider your priorities, the more you can align them with your purpose, the greater your fulfillment.

Priorities

1. You can tell what is important to people by where they spend their money and time.

2. Efficiency is doing things right. Effectiveness is doing the right things.

3. Master this process:

    » Evaluate: Is this the best thing?

    » Delegate: What can I take off my plate?

    » Estimate: How much time is required?

4. Focus your energy on activities that give you the greatest return.

Following these steps will help you live by your priorities:

1. Find a mentor/accountability partner. Write two possibilities.

_____

_____

_____

_____

_____

_____

2. What are activities that you can delegate?

_____

_____

_____

_____

_____

_____

_____

_____

Step Five: Priorities

3. What activities can you eliminate?

_____

_____

_____

_____

4. Write your three "top priority tasks" for the day (your priorities will change every day). Before writing, ask yourself, "If I absolutely knew I could accomplish three important priorities today, what would they be?" Write them down, then focus your energy and time on those things. Always ask yourself: Do these priorities align with my purpose?

_____

_____

_____

_____

> ## "Successful people live by priorities, not by pressure."
>
> **Quest of the Keys**

— 11 —
Step Six: Gratitude

"It is impossible to feel grateful and depressed in the same moment."

Naomi Williams

Being Grateful—The Little Things
Experiences happen every day that can teach us valuable lessons—especially about being grateful. Sometimes we are too busy to take the time to learn from them. I have lots of room to grow in all areas. What about you?

I want to share an experience that happened during Christmas. My wife and I found out about a mom and dad who had three precious boys and were not going to be able to buy any Christmas presents. We decided to put a big tin of popcorn and some Christmas candy in a bag. We also tied a gift card to the top so they could go shopping and buy gifts. When the mom saw the bag with the popcorn and candy inside, she was totally thrilled, not even seeing the gift card. My thought was, *How can you be excited about the popcorn and candy when you still do not have gifts to give your children?* Needless to say, she was speechless when she found the gift card.

Since that day, I try to remember to be grateful for the little things. In fact, every day, I write down three things I am grateful for. I have found this to be helpful in being grateful. It is also a way to have a better perspective on life.

The Importance of Being Grateful

When you keep a list of what you are thankful for, it can help you do these things:

- Feel happier.

- Become more optimistic about life.

- Experience longer and better sleep.

- Increase physical and mental well-being, which in turn increases energy levels.

- Have more friends and better relationships.

The Secret to Happiness

The secret to being happy is not a new home or a new car; in fact, it is not anything new. Not a new job or a new vacation; not even marrying your dream guy or gal.

Research shows happiness comes from gratitude. Harvard Health Publications notes this research on gratitude. Two psychologists, Dr. Robert A. Emmons of the University of California, Davis and Dr. Michael E. McCullough of the University of Miami found that people who focused more on gratitude than on aggravation were more optimistic, felt better about their lives, and were happier. Surprisingly, they also exercised more and had fewer visits to physicians than those who focused on the negative.

Ways to Cultivate Gratitude

GRACE—Give people grace (giving something free the person may not deserve).

RECOGNITION—Everyone likes to be recognized!

APPRECIATION—Show people your appreciation.

THANK-YOU—A simple thank-you communicates gratitude and respect.

INVOLVEMENT—Giving your time to a person shows gratitude.

TALK LESS—Ask people about their lives; it communicates gratitude.

UNDERSTANDING—Be understanding; you never know what a person is going through.

DEMONSTRATE—How much you value others.

ENCOURAGEMENT—Everyone needs it, and everyone can give it.

Instead of complaining, choose to be thankful. Let me suggest that you take an inventory of all the things you are grateful for in your life. It will improve your attitude!

> "When I started counting my blessings, my whole life turned around."
>
> **Willie Nelson**

Responding to the following will help you focus on gratitude:

1. List three things that made you smile today.

_____

_____

_____

_____

2. Name three people in your life you can turn to for comfort or support.

_____

_____

_____

_____

Step Six: Gratitude

3. Name three things you like about your job/place you live, etc.

4. How did you serve someone today?

5. List three things you are grateful for today.

_____

_____

_____

_____

6. Repeat #5 each day on your 3x5 card.

> "Gratitude blocks toxic emotions such as envy, resentment, regret, and depression, which can destroy our happiness."
>
> **Robert Emmons**

–12–

3x5 in Review

Step 1: Purpose .... stays the same each day.

Step 2: Passion .... stays the same each day.

Step 3: Yearly Goals .... stay the same each day.

Step 4: Daily Disciplines .... stay the same each day.

Step 5: Priorities .... change each day.

Step 6: Gratitude .... changes each day.

You may ask, "Why write down your purpose, passion, goals, and disciplines each day, when they do not change?"

GREATER...

Clarity,

Focus,

Results!

Practical Suggestions That Really Work

- Each day, write the date on a new index card or page in the note section of your phone or computer.

- Always keep your written plan close; you may want to look back over it during the day.

- Keep your written plan from day to day, year to year. You may want to review the plan monthly, share your results with others, or remember to be grateful!

- Complete your written plan at the same time each day. (It works well for me to do my work early in the morning.)

Why do you need paper? Before you go to the index card or phone, you must work through your purpose and plans by writing them down on paper. Once you have thought about each area, transfer everything to the index card or app.

What next? Begin!

It could take a few hours or a few days to develop your plan. Then take 10-15 minutes a day to fill out the ideas for *Life on a 3x5*.

Over the years, I have worked with thousands of leaders, CEOs, general managers, pastors, military leaders, executive directors, entrepreneurs, educators, politicians, administrators, writers, speakers, etc. Some experienced an 800% improvement, and some stayed the same. Why the difference?

Commitment and Application!

Some had a much higher degree of commitment than others. Some had a greater understanding of how to apply the things I taught.

What am I saying? It is now up to you to do your part!

Share Your Success

The fact that you have a personal growth plan puts you ahead of 99% of the people in the world. I encourage you to share your success with others around you. Know that I am pulling for you and am very proud of you for joining the army of people who have decided to bring personal development into their lives.

Continue to Learn and Grow

- For Scotty's online training *Life on a 3x5: A Framework For Daily Success Program*, go to ScottySanders.com/lifeona3x5.

- To bring Scotty in to train and/or speak to your organization or company, go to ScottySanders.com.

- To get a copy of Scotty's *Quest of the Keys* book or learn how you can support Character Education in schools, go to QuestoftheKeys.org.

"Live well, lead well, finish well!"

Scotty Sanders